DAISY DAYDREAM
BUS RHYMES AND JOKES

What did the bus driver say to the frog?

Hop on

Sue Wickstead

Published in 2019 by Sue Wickstead
ISBN: 978-0-9930737-9-3

Written by Sue Wickstead
Illustrations by Artful Doodlers
Layout design by Claire Shaw

© Sue Wickstead 2019
All rights reserved. No part of this publication may be reproduced in any form.

DAISY DAYDREAM
BUS RHYMES AND JOKES

SUE WICKSTEAD

*To my brother David, who thought
Daisy needed a few rhymes to share
and jokes to make him giggle*

CONTENTS

The Bus by Helen Price	7
It's the Playbus	8
The Wheels on the Bus	9
Humpty Dumpty	10
Little Miss Muffet	10
Little Bo Peep	11
There was an Old Woman	12
Baa Baa Black Sheep	14
Jack and Jill	15
Incy Wincy Spider	15
Elly's Cat	16
Daisy	17
A Playbus Song	18
Jay-Jay the Supersonic Bus	20
Jay-Jay at the Airport	22
Bus Colours	23
A Playbus Journey	24
The Christmas Bus	26

```
Does this bus stop
at the river?

If it doesn't there
will be a very big splash!
```
Child Return

Why did the bus stop?

Because he saw the zebra crossing.

Child Return

Why did the bat miss the bus?

Because he hung about too long.

Child — Return — 10:56am

Adult Single

What sport can you play on the bus?

Squash

What is red, runs on wheels and eats grass?

A bus — I lied about the grass!

How do eels get around the seabed?
They go by octobus.

THE BUS
By Helen Price

What a clamour!
What a fuss!
Getting on and off a bus.
Pushing, squeezing,
Stamping, nudging.
Never was there
So much budging.

"Quick!" says mother,
"There's another".
Father answers,
"Don't be silly!
That one goes to Piccadilly".

IT'S THE PLAYBUS!

But where does it go?
Where does it stop?
What's the sign on the lollipop?
... It's the playbus stop!
(It's Jay-Jay's stop)

Child Return

Do buses and trains run on time?

Usually, yes.

No, they don't - buses run on wheels and trains run on tracks.

Adult Single

What is the difference between a bus driver and a cold?

A bus driver knows the stops and a cold stops the nose.

THE WHEELS ON THE BUS

The children on the bus
they play and play,
play and play, play and play.
The children on the bus
they play and play all day long.
(And have lots of fun!).

The wheels on the bus is an American folk song written by Verna Hills – published in 1939

HUMPTY DUMPTY

Humpty Dumpty sat on the wall,
Humpty Dumpty felt such a fool!
He's used all the paint
and he's used all the glue
now Humpty Dumpty has nothing to do!!

LITTLE MISS MUFFET

Little Miss Muffet
sat by the slide,
under the tree she thought
she could hide.
Down came a spider
on a long golden thread,
Miss Muffet, she saw it
and homeward she fled.

LITTLE BO PEEP

Little Bo Peep,
can't get any sleep.
She doesn't know
what to do.

The children are sad
the weather is bad
then along comes
the playbus. Phew!

With its toys to play
each and every day
there is always
something new.

Cross-eyed Monster: When I grow up, I want to be a bus driver.
BUS TICKET BUS TICKET BUS TICKET BUS TICKET BUS TICKET BUS TICKET BUS TICKET BUS TICKET BUS TICKET BU

Witch: Well I won't stand in your way.

THERE WAS AN OLD WOMAN

There was an old woman
who lived on a bus.
She had so many children
who made such a fuss.

So she gave them some paint
and she gave them some glue.
Now there's plenty of things
for the children to do!
(And they are happy now.)

BAA BAA BLACK SHEEP

Baa Baa Black Sheep,
may we have some wool?
To give to the children
the playbus is quite full.

We could use it on our pictures,
on our model made with glue.
Maybe weave a clever pattern
especially for you.

All the colours of the rainbow,
blue and red and green.
To make a special picture
the best you've ever seen.

JACK AND JILL

Jack and Jill,
went to town
riding on the bus.
They bumped along
and sang a song
making such a fuss.

INCY WINCY SPIDER

Incy Wincy Spider
climbed up the bus.
Down came the rain
and made poor Incy fuss.
Out came the sunshine
that dried up all the rain.
So Incy Wincy spider
climbed up the bus again.

ELLY'S CAT

Mary had a little lamb
but Elly had a cat.
Everywhere that Elly went
that's where the cat was at!
It followed to the bus one day
and joined in all the fun.
It made the children laugh and play
amusing everyone!

DAISY

Daisy, Daisy, the children all love you,
they go crazy, whenever you come in view.

There's so much to keep them busy,
they won't get in a tizzy.
The parents smile and sit awhile
because they love you, too.

A PLAYBUS SONG

Sing a song for playbus,
a playbus full of toys
with children playing merrily
making such a noise.

The bus is full of books and games,
and songs the children sing.
Where children and their families
can do most anything.

It really is a lot of fun,
no matter where we go,
so why not come along to play,
and then you're sure to know.

Did you say you fell over fifty feet but didn't hurt yourself?

Yes — I was trying to get to the back of the bus.

Passenger: Does this bus go to London?

Driver: No

Passenger: But it says London on the front.

Driver: There's an advertisement for baked beans on the side, but we don't sell them!

 Alex left work after a tiring day. Take the bus home, suggested a friend. My mother would only make me take it back, said Alex.

Child — Single —3:30pm

Driver: What have I got in my hands?

Passenger: A double-decker bus!

Driver: You looked!

Child Return

JAY-JAY THE SUPERSONIC BUS

A flash of colour darting by,
lifting high towards the sky.

'Why not me?' poor Jay-Jay sighed,
I've tried the speed bumps,
tried and tried.

It doesn't matter how fast I go
I cannot fly, I'm far too slow.

If only I had fitted wings
instead I'm filled with toys and things.

Oh well! I suppose it doesn't matter
the toys would only fall and clatter.

So, instead of flying far away,
my children just have to come and play.

JAY-JAY AT THE AIRPORT

There was a bus in days gone by
who really wished that he could fly.

Beside the runway he would race,
keeping up their pre-flight pace.

He'd watch the planes racing past
lift to the sky and flying fast.

Where do they go, he'd like to know?
They were fast and he was slow.

He tried to use the roadway bumps
to lift him up and help him jump.

If only he had outstretched wings
instead he's filled with toys and things.

Oh well, he thought, it doesn't matter
my toys and games would fall and clatter.

His little visitors came to play,
with holidays not far away.

A summer of fun with lots of art,
the playbus certainly plays a part.

Jay-Jay leaves for another year,
but he will return so have no fear.

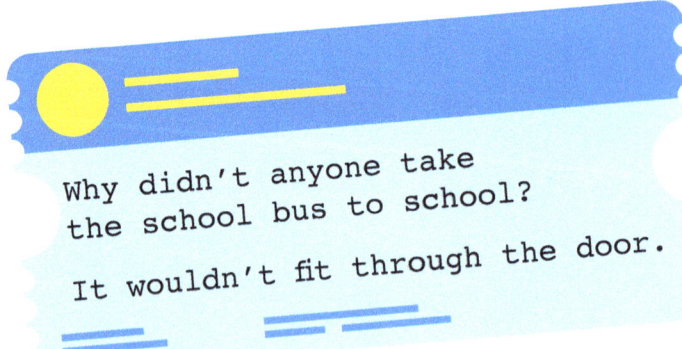

Why didn't anyone take the school bus to school?

It wouldn't fit through the door.

BUS COLOURS

Red bus,   green bus,   yellow bus,   blue.

Off on a journey
just for you.

Never mind the weather,
sun, rain or snow.
The bus always takes you
where you want to go.

A PLAYBUS JOURNEY

A journey on a playbus
is a different road to take.
You don't have to sit in silence,
there's lots of things to make.

You can paint or draw a picture,
and even play with sand.
In your imagination,
you fly to a fantasy land.

You can dress up in a costume,
pretend to be a king.
Inside the bus there's lots to do –
you can do almost anything.

You can sit and listen quietly
to a story from a book.
The playbus is amazing
so why not take a look?

THE CHRISTMAS BUS

Took the bus to Bethlehem
bumping all the way.
Should have gone by donkey
but that would take all day.

Elly: What's the difference between a cake and a school bus?

Tom: I don't know.

Elly: I'm glad I didn't send you to pick up my birthday cake!

Adult Single

What bus crossed the ocean?

Columbus

Adult Single

Have you heard that all buses are stopping today?

No, is there a strike?

No, we are stopping to let the passengers off.

What is a bus?

A bus is a vehicle that goes twice as fast when you run after it than when you are in it.

BUS TICKET

Passenger: Will this bus take me to London?

Driver: Which part?

Passenger: All of me of course!

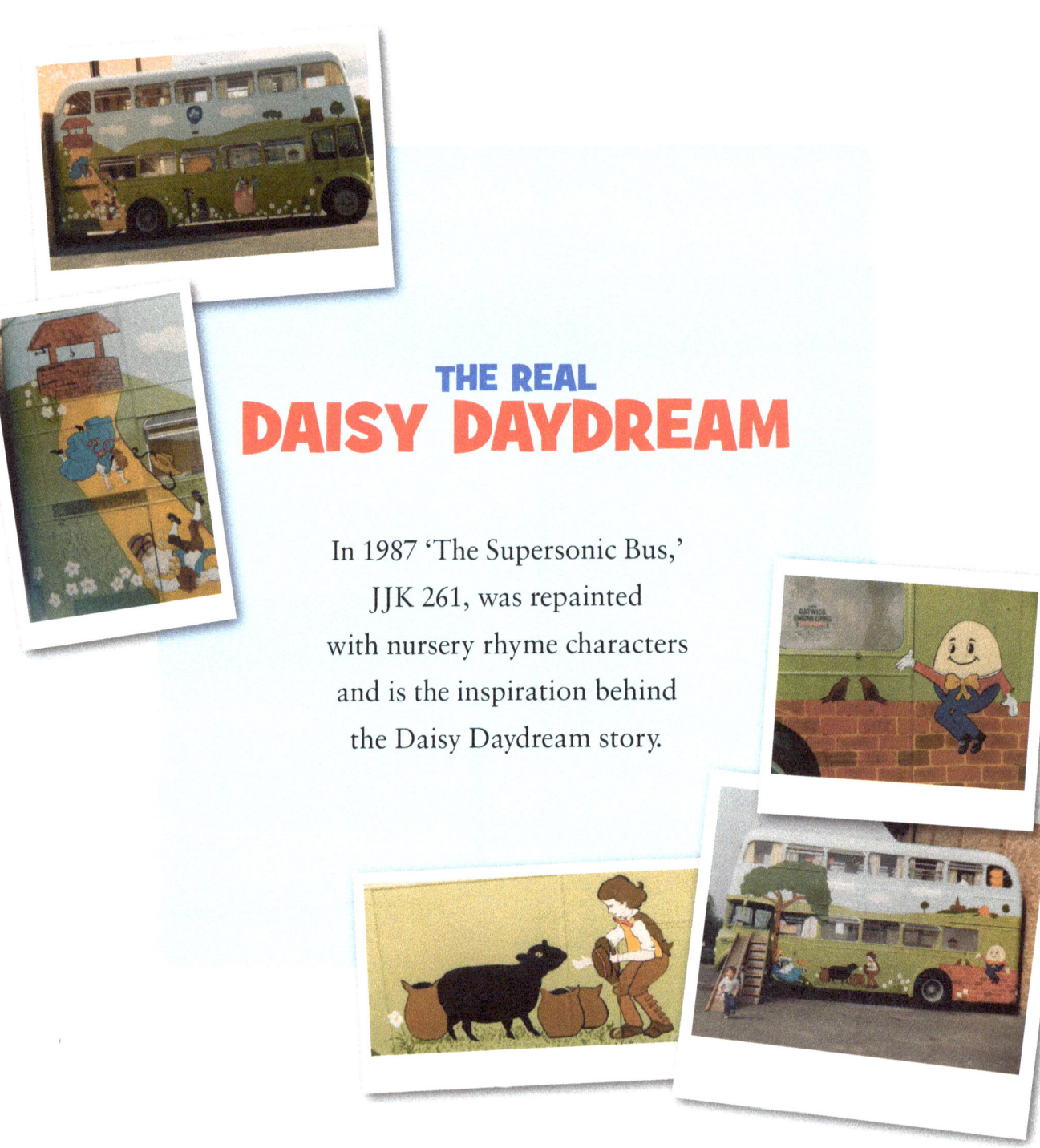

THE REAL
DAISY DAYDREAM

In 1987 'The Supersonic Bus,' JJK 261, was repainted with nursery rhyme characters and is the inspiration behind the Daisy Daydream story.

Books by Sue Wickstead

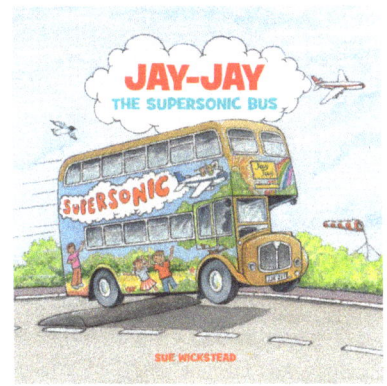
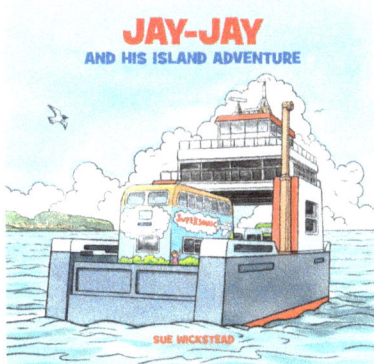
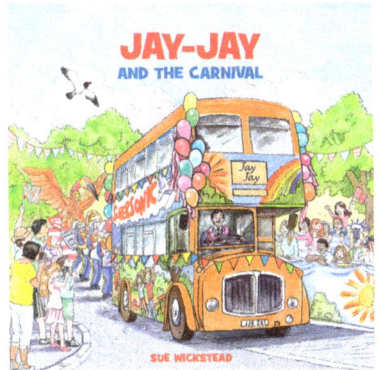
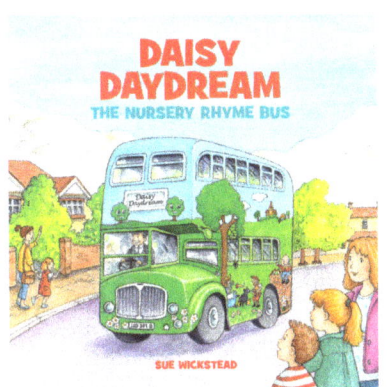
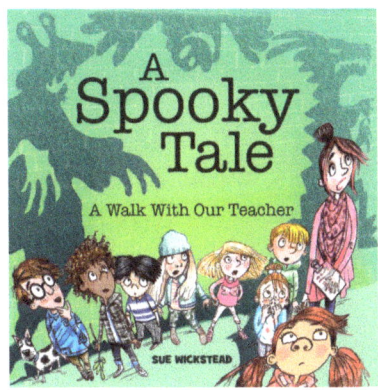
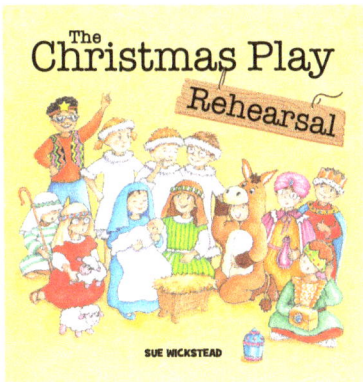

Sue Wickstead is an author and Primary School teacher working across Sussex and Surrey. For over twenty years, alongside her teaching career, she has worked with a children's charity, The Bewbush Playbus Association, which inspired the Jay-Jay series of books. www.suewickstead.co.uk

www.ingramcontent.com/pod-product-compliance
Lightning Source LLC
Chambersburg PA
CBHW040752020526
44118CB00042B/2924